Marsupials
Wombats

by Natalie Deniston

Bullfrog Books

Ideas for Parents and Teachers

Bullfrog Books let children practice reading informational text at the earliest reading levels. Repetition, familiar words, and photo labels support early readers.

Before Reading
- Discuss the cover photo. What does it tell them?
- Look at the picture glossary together. Read and discuss the words.

Read the Book
- "Walk" through the book and look at the photos. Let the child ask questions. Point out the photo labels.
- Read the book to the child, or have them read independently.

After Reading
- Prompt the child to think more. Ask: Wombats are marsupials. Moms have pouches. Can you name any other marsupials?

Bullfrog Books are published by Jump!
5357 Penn Avenue South
Minneapolis, MN 55419
www.jumplibrary.com

Copyright © 2025 Jump! International copyright reserved in all countries. No part of this book may be reproduced in any form without written permission from the publisher.

Library of Congress Cataloging-in-Publication Data

Names: Deniston, Natalie, author.
Title: Wombats / by Natalie Deniston.
Description: Minneapolis, MN: Jump!, Inc., [2025]
Series: Marsupials | Includes index.
Audience: Ages 5–8
Identifiers: LCCN 2024020097 (print)
LCCN 2024020098 (ebook)
ISBN 9798892135313 (hardcover)
ISBN 9798892135320 (paperback)
ISBN 9798892135337 (ebook)
Subjects: LCSH: Wombats—Juvenile literature.
Classification: LCC QL737.M39 D46 2025 (print)
LCC QL737.M39 (ebook)
DDC 599.2/4—dc23/eng/20240507
LC record available at https://lccn.loc.gov/2024020097
LC ebook record available at https://lccn.loc.gov/2024020098

Editor: Katie Chanez
Designer: Emma Almgren-Bersie

Photo Credits: imageBROKER.com GmbH & Co. KG/Alamy, cover; Benny Marty/Shutterstock, 1; Marco Tomasini/Shutterstock, 3; karenfoleyphotography/Shutterstock, 4; Maik Boenig/Shutterstock, 5, 23tr; Sonijya/Shutterstock, 6–7, 23tl; Zita Stankova/Dreamstime, 8; phototrip/iStock, 9; 3sby/Shutterstock, 10–11, 23br; ozflash/iStock, 12–13, 19; Tom Wayman/Shutterstock, 14–15, 23bl; William Edge/Shutterstock, 16–17; Animals Animals/SuperStock, 18; ooodles/Shutterstock, 20–21; Gerry Pearce/Alamy, 22; andrewburgess/iStock, 24.

Printed in the United States of America at Corporate Graphics in North Mankato, Minnesota.

Table of Contents

Dig and Chew	4
Parts of a Wombat	22
Picture Glossary	23
Index	24
To Learn More	24

Dig and Chew

A wombat digs.

It makes a burrow.

burrow

It blocks the burrow.
With what?
Its butt!

It sleeps during the day.

It wakes up at night.

joey

Mom has a pouch!
A joey is in it.
It faces back.

Mom digs.
Dirt flies.
The joey is safe.

The joey grows. It comes out of the pouch.

It grows up.
It looks for food.
It eats plants.

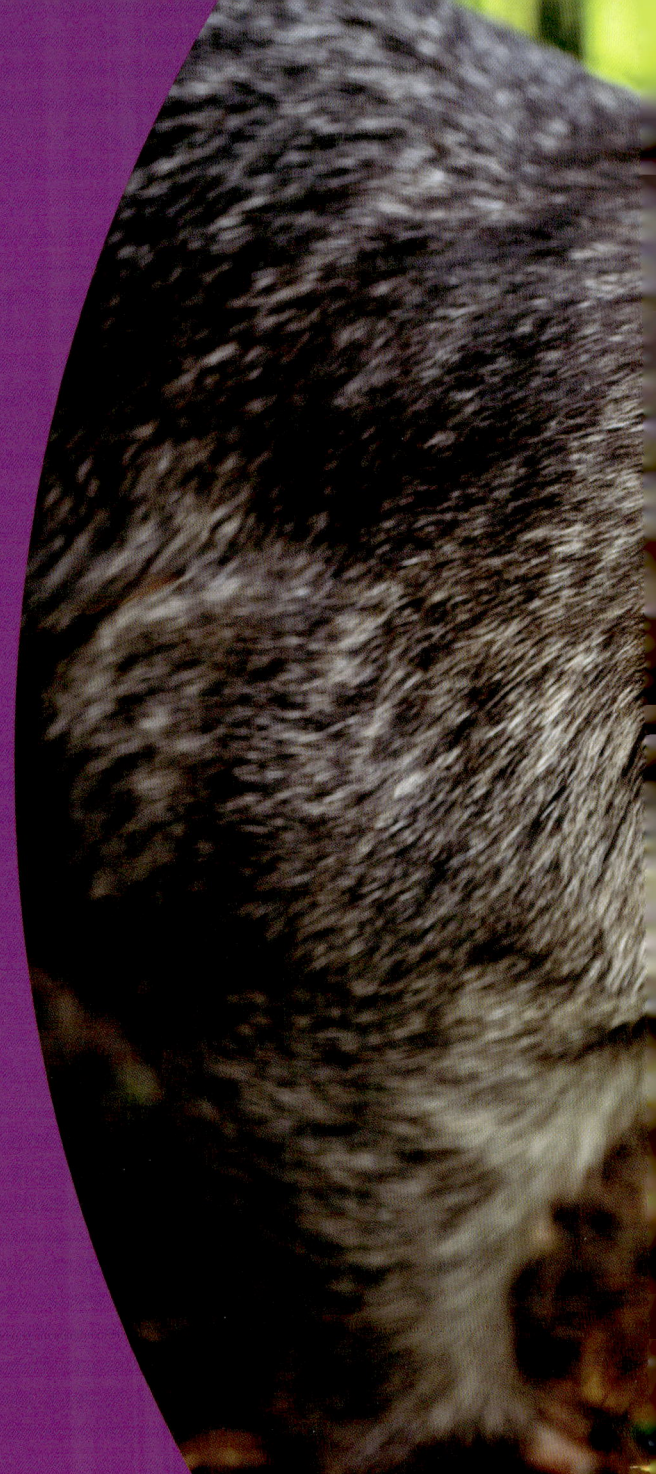

It chews wood. Why?

This keeps its teeth short.

teeth

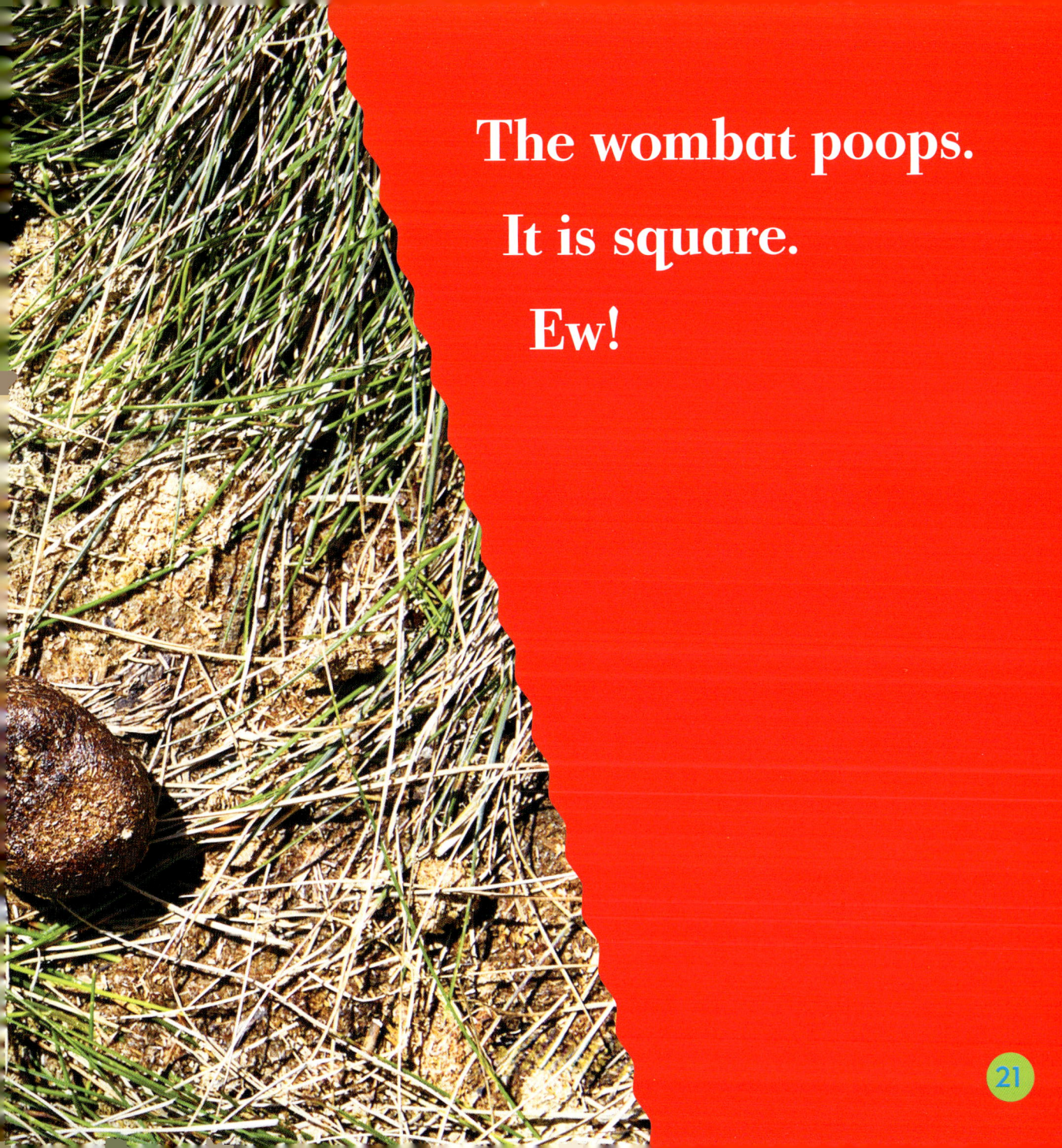

The wombat poops.
It is square.
Ew!

Parts of a Wombat

What are the parts of a wombat? Take a look!

Picture Glossary

blocks
Stops something.

burrow
The home of a wild animal.

joey
A baby wombat.

pouch
A pocket in a marsupial mother's body in which it carries its young.

Index

blocks 6
burrow 5, 6
chews 18
digs 4, 12
eats 16
grows 15, 16
joey 11, 12, 15
plants 16
poops 21
pouch 11, 15
sleeps 8
teeth 19

To Learn More

Finding more information is as easy as 1, 2, 3.

① Go to www.factsurfer.com
② Enter "wombats" into the search box.
③ Choose your book to see a list of websites.